How to Play
FIELDING

Edited & Compiled by

Dr. Samir R. Pawar
B.P.Ed., M.A. (English), M.P.Ed., M.Phil.,
Ph.D. (Physical Education)
Visiting Lecturer
Rashtrasant Tukadoji Maharaj Nagpur University
(Maharashtra)

PRERNA PRAKASHAN
C-13, Plot No. D-5, Rose Apartment,
Sector-14 Extension, Rohini, Delhi-110085
Phones: (Office) 011-65749511, 23240261
(Mobile) 9868028838 (Residence) 27562163
E-mail: lakshaythani@hotmail.com

Published by:

PRERNA PRAKASHAN
C-13, Plot No. D-5, Rose Apartment,
Sector-14 Extension, Rohini, Delhi-110085
Ph. : (Office) 65749511, 23240261 (Mobile) 9868028838
(Residence) 27562163 (Fax) 011-23240261
E-mail: *lakshaythani@hotmail.com*

I.S.B.N: 978-93-81867-49-5

PRINTED IN INDIA 2013

Laser Typeset by:
JAIN MEDIA GRAPHICS,
C-8/77-B, Keshav Puram, Delhi-35

Printed by:
CHAWLA OFFSET PRINTERS, Delhi-110052

Price: Rs. 250/-

CONTENTS

1

FIELDING— AN INTRODUCTION

Fielding in the sport of cricket is the action of fielders in collecting the ball after it is struck by the batsman, in such a way either to limit the number of runs that the batsman scores or to get the batsman out by catching

the ball in flight or running the batsman out. Cricket fielding position can be broken down into offside and legside parts of the field.

A fielder or fieldsman may field the ball with any part of his person. However, if while the ball is in play he wilfully fields it otherwise (e.g., by using his hat), the ball becomes dead and 5 penalty runs are awarded to the batting side unless the ball previously struck a batsman not attempting to hit or avoid the ball. Most of the rules covering fielders are in Law 41 of the Laws of cricket.

In the early days of Test cricket, fielding was not a priority and many players were sloppy when it came to fielding. With the advent of One Day International matches, fielding became more professional as saving runs became more important. A good fielding side can often save 30+ runs in the course of an ODI innings.

Fielding in Cricket is a ancient sports which is originally discovered in England and later developed and spread all over the world including Europe,

Australia, USA and particularly in Asia. It is the most famous sport which has rapidly spread all over the world and gained its popularity at peak after soccer being the first famous world sport.

Fielding is just as important and can be just as attractive as batting or bowling. Many matches are won or lost as much by the standard of fielding, as by the actual strength of the batting or the bowling. What is more delightful to watch is a fielding side which by initiative, concentration and anticipation, dismisses batsmen by brilliant catching, and which displays consistently safe and clean handling to prevent run, and speedy and accurate returns to the wicket to effect run outs.

A fielder should go to the position desired by his Captain or bowler and stay there. He should not stray about. Remember, the bowler is bowling to the field he has set, not to the one to which the fielders have wandered.

After going to his allotted place in the field, he should show an intelligent interest in the game and expect every ball bowled to be hit to him. He should try to anticipate the batsman's stroke and keep an eye on his Captain. He may wish to move him without the batsman knowing.

Fielder should be ready to move to his next position at the end of an over. If the fielder is instructed to field on the boundary, then he should go to the boundary and not stand ten yards inside it. It is easier to run forward to take a catch than to run backwards, and it is also easier to narrow the angle to cut off a boundary hit from the boundary line than from a position ten yards inside it. The first and second slip fielders should watch

the ball from the bowlers hand on to the bat, and the third slip and gully, being wider, should watch the bat.

All the fielders near the wicket should once they are down in a half crouching positions, stay there until they either have to field the ball or until it has reached the wicket-keeper or been played away. Those fielders away from the wicket, on the other hand, will start to move in as the bowler approaches the wicket. The ball should always be returned to the wicket-keeper, unless the fielder is close to the bowler.

Once the ball is in wicket-keeper's hand, it is dead. If a ball is thrown at the wicket-keeper, the fielder near and behind the wicket-keeper should always back up, in case the keeper misses the ball or the thrower makes a wide throw. There is nothing so annoying as a bad throwing that lands outside the wicket-keeper's reach and, because no fielder has backed up, causes extra runs.

When a ball is thrown at the bowler's end, it is the duty of the fielders near that wicket to rush up and gather the ball to make a run out. A bowler should be saved from taking fast throws as there is a possibility of his getting hurt which would make him unfit to bowl effectively or take further part in the game. Be careful with the new ball. Always return it full toss. Do not let it hit the ground.

A good fielder will enjoy his cricket and can get a great deal of satisfaction when he comes off the field if he knows he has saved runs for his side or made a catch which may prove a match winner.

Cricket is being played on a circular or an oval-shaped field. The area situated at the centre of the field is called the pitch. At the both end of the cricket pitch, two sets of wickets are situated. Three sets of vertical sticks together are called the wicket. Normally, a wicket is about 6-7 inches in breadth and about 3 feet in length.

The cricket pitch is designed and constructed in such a manner that it can afford the bounce generated by the cricket ball. The equator of the ball consisted of the seam of the ball. The bat which is an important instrument of a batsman is a paddle shaped instrument which is used by the batsmen in order to hit the ball thrown by the bowlers. Normally, batsmen used to choose their bats of their own style which is convenient and easier for them to play with.

There are three important ingredients of cricket viz., Batting, Bowling and Fielding. All have equal importance of their own. By the mixture of these three aspects, the sport of cricket is played. The players having good efficiency in batting skills are usually called the

batsmen. While the players having excellent skills in the bowling are usually called the bowlers. On the other hand, there are players in the cricket sport who used to perfect in fielding skills are called as fielders. There are at least one specialist fielders who is called a wicketkeeper, four specialist bowlers and 5-6 specialist batsmen in a team side.

In the sport of cricket, the only one area in which all the cricketers should be efficient is the Fielding. Usually all the players either batsmen or bowlers have to equally field in the cricket. A batsman used to field when he is not batting, similarly, a bowler too has to field when he is not bowling.

Basically, there are two types of fielding which are planned by the two teams in cricket viz., close-in fielding and in the deep fielding. The close-in fielding is very similar to those in baseball called playing the infield. While the in the deep fielding resemble to the playing the outfield.

Usually, the close-in fielders used to stand at the distance of 10 feet from the batsman crease. No fielders other than wicketkeeper used to wear hand gloves and safety helmets.

The only objective of the fielders is to stop the ball hit by the batsman or from any sources i.e., leg byes, byes, over throw etc. The other objective of the fielders other than stopping the ball is to get the batsman out. The batsman will be called out by the field umpire if he plays loose stroke in the air and a fielder catches the ball, if the batsman is running between the wickets in order to get run and he is unsafe at the popping crease with the bat in the air he is declared out by the umpire. Thus, the fielders play their important role in order to cease the batsman from playing a long innings.

2

FIELDING POSITIONS

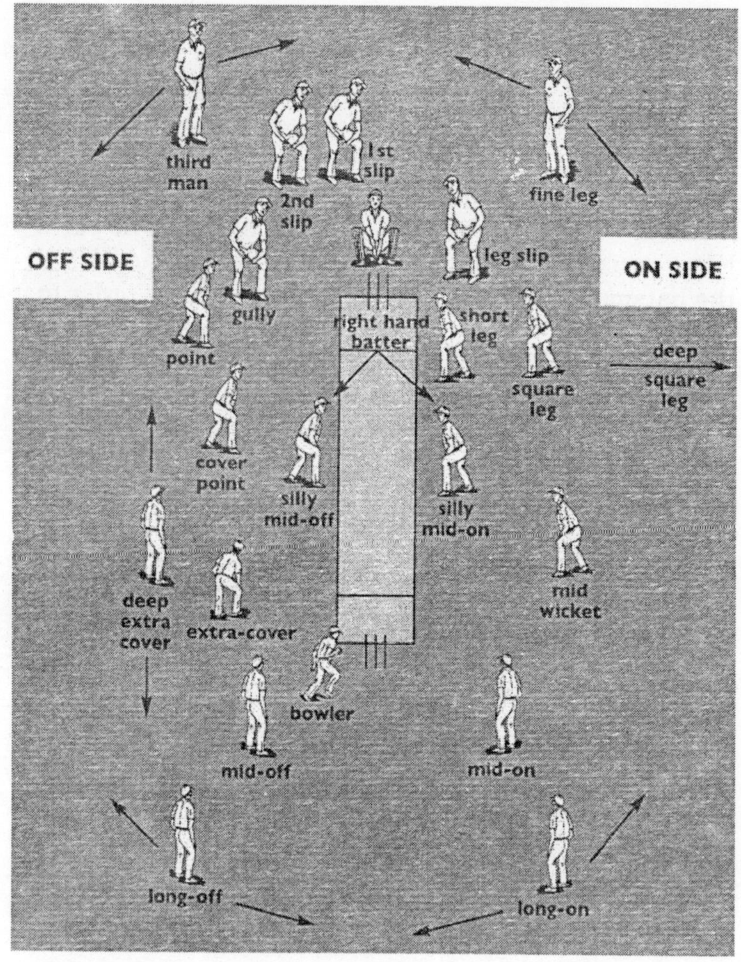

Since there are only 11 players on a team, one of whom is the bowler, and usually another as the wicket-keeper, at most nine other fielding positions can be used at any given time. Which positions are filled by players and which remain vacant is a tactical decision made by the captain of the fielding team. The captain (usually in consultation with the bowler and sometimes other members of the team) may move players between fielding positions at any time except when a bowler is in the act of bowling to a batsman.

There are a number of named basic fielding positions, some of which are employed very commonly and others that are used less often. However, fielding positions are not fixed, and fielders can be placed in positions that differ from the basic positions. Most of the positions are named roughly according to a system of polar coordinates - one word (leg, cover, mid-wicket) specifies the angle from the batsman, and is optionally preceded by an adjective describing the distance from the batsman (silly, short, deep or long). Words such as "backward", "forward", or "square" can further indicate the angle.

The image shows the location of most of the named fielding positions. This image assumes the batsman is right-handed. The area to the left of a right-handed batsman (from the batsman's point of view - facing the bowler) is called the leg side or on side, while that to the right is the off side. If the batsman is left-handed, the leg and off sides are reversed and the fielding positions are a mirror image of those shown.

CATCHING POSITIONS

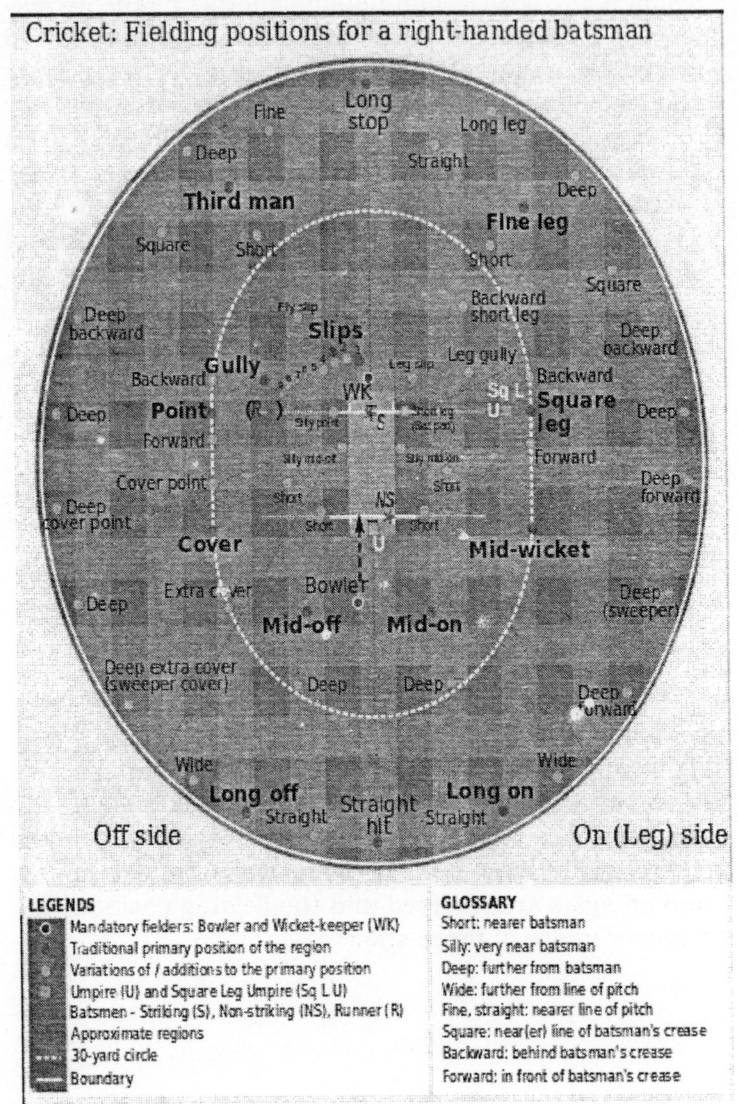

Some fielding positions are used offensively. That is, players are put there with the main aim being to catch out the batsman rather than to stop or slow down the scoring of runs. These positions include Slip (often there are multiple slips next to each other, designated First slip, Second slip, Third slip, etc., numbered outwards from the wicket-keeper) meant to catch balls that just edge off the bat; Fly slip; Gully; Leg slip; Leg gully; the short and silly positions. Bat pad is a position specifically intended to catch balls that unintentionally strike the bat and leg pad, and thus end up only a metre or two to the leg side.

OTHER POSITIONS

Other positions worth noting include:

- Wicket-keeper
- Long stop, who stands behind the wicket-keeper towards the boundary (usually when a wicket-keeper is believed to be inept and almost never seen in professional cricket). This position is sometimes euphemistically referred to as very fine leg.
- Sweeper, an alternative name for deep cover, deep extra cover or deep midwicket (that is, near the boundary on the off side or the on side), usually defensive and intended to prevent a four being scored.
- Cow corner, an informal jocular term for the position on the boundary between deep midwicket and long on.
- 45 on the 1. A position on the leg side 45° behind square, defending the single. An alternative description for backward short leg.
- Also the bowler, after delivering the ball, must avoid running on the pitch so usually ends up fielding near

silly mid on or silly mid off, but somewhat closer to the pitch.

Modifiers

Deep, long

Farther away from the batsman.

Short

Closer to the batsman.

Silly

Very close to the batsman, so-called because of the perceived danger of doing so.

Square

Somewhere along an imaginary extension of the popping crease.

Fine

Closer to an extension of an imaginary line along the middle of the pitch bisecting the stumps, when describing a fielder behind square.

Straight

Closer to an extension of an imaginary line along the middle of the pitch bisecting the stumps, when describing a fielder in front of square.

Wide

Further from an extension of an imaginary line along the middle of the pitch bisecting the stumps.

Forward

In front of square; further towards the end occupied by the bowler and further away from the end occupied by the batsman on strike.

Backward

Behind square; further towards the end occupied by the batsman on strike and further away from the end occupied by the bowler.

Additionally, commentators or spectators discussing the details of field placement will often use descriptive phrases such as "gully is a bit wider than normal" or "mid off is standing too deep, he should come in shorter".

Restrictions on Field Placement

Fielders may be placed anywhere on the field, subject to the following rules. At the time the ball is bowled:

• No fielder may be standing on or with any part of his body over the pitch (the central strip of the playing area between the wickets). If his body casts a shadow over the pitch the shadow must not move until after the batsman has played (or had the opportunity to play) at the ball.

• There may be no more than two fielders, other than the wicket-keeper, standing in the quadrant of the field behind square leg. See Bodyline for details on one reason this rule exists.

• In some one-day matches:

• During designated overs of an innings, there may be no more than two fielders standing outside an oval line marked on the field, being semicircles centred on the middle stump of each wicket of radius 30 yards, joined by straight lines parallel to the pitch. This is known as the fielding circle. In addition, during these overs there must be two fielders (other than the wicket-keeper) in designated "close catching" positions.

For the remainder of the innings there may be no more than four fielders standing outside the fielding circle.

In addition no fielder may stand behind directly behind the wicketkeeper. Fielders may be placed anywhere on the field other than the pitch or behind the wicketkeeper.

The restriction for one-day cricket is designed to prevent the fielding team from setting extremely defensive fields and concentrating solely on preventing the batting team from scoring runs.

If any of these rules is violated, an umpire will call the delivery a no ball. Additionally a player may not make any significant movement after the ball comes into play and before the ball reaches the striker. If this happens, an umpire will call and signal 'dead ball'. For close fielders anything other than minor adjustments to stance or position in relation to the striker is significant. In the outfield, fielders may move in towards the striker or striker's wicket; indeed, they usually do. However, anything other than slight movement off line or away from the striker is to be considered significant.

Tactics of Field Placement

With only nine fielders (apart from the bowler and wicket-keeper), the captain of the fielding team must decide which fielding positions to cover, and which to leave vacant. The placement of fielders is one of the major tactical considerations for the fielding captain.

Attacking and Defending

The main decision for a fielding captain is to strike a balance between setting an attacking field and a

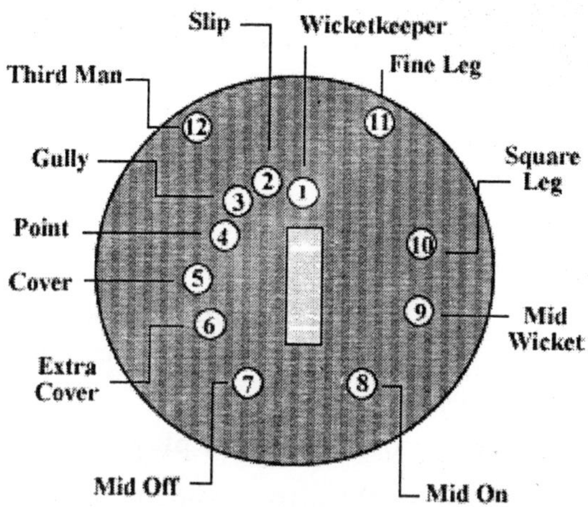

defensive field. An attacking field is one in which fielders are positioned in such a way that they are likely to take catches, and thus likely to get the batsman out. Such a field generally involves having many fielders close to the batsman, especially behind the batsman in either slip or short leg positions.

A defensive field is one in which most of the field is covered by a fielder; the batsman will therefore find it hard to score large numbers of runs. This generally involves having many fielders far from the batsman and in front of him, in the positions where he is most likely to hit the ball.

Many factors govern the decisions on field placements, including: the tactical situation in the match; which bowler is bowling; how long the batsman has been in; the wear on the ball; the state of the wicket; the light; or even how close you are to an interval in play.

Some general principles:

Attack...

...new batsmen

A batsman early in his innings is more likely to make a miscalculated or rash shot, so it pays to have catching fielders ready.

...with the new ball

Fast bowlers get the most swing and bounce with a newer ball, factors that make it harder to bat without making an error.

...when returning from a break in play

Batsmen must settle into a batting rhythm again when resuming play for a new session or after drinks, bad weather, or injury interrupt a session. While doing so, they are more likely to make mistakes.

...with quality bowlers

A team's best bowlers tend to deliver the most difficult balls to hit, so they get the most benefit from the support of an attacking field.

...when the pitch helps the bowler

A moist pitch helps fast bowlers get unpredictable seam-movement of the ball, while a dry, crumbling pitch helps spin bowlers get unpredictable spin and damp, overcast conditions help swing bowlers. All three situations can lead to catches flying to close attacking fielders.

...when the batting team is under pressure

If the batting team is doing poorly or has low morale, increase the pressure by attacking with the field.

...when the batting side are playing for a draw

when a team is a long way behind in a first-class game and there is not much time left to play, it becomes more important to bowl out the side and finish the game than to control runs.

Defend...

...when batsmen are settled in

It is difficult to get batsmen out when they have been batting for a long time and are comfortable with the bowling. The best tactic is often to defend and force the run scoring rate to slow down, which can frustrate the batsman into playing a rash shot.

...when the batting team needs to score runs quickly

In situations where the batting team must score quickly in order to win or press an advantage (because, for example, a limited-overs innings is ending soon), slowing down the scoring becomes more important than trying to dismiss the batsmen.

...when the batting team is scoring quickly

If the batsmen are managing to score runs quickly, it is unlikely they are offering many chances to get them out, so reduce the run scoring rate.

...when the ball and pitch offer no help to the bowlers

If there is no movement of the ball and the batsmen can hit it comfortably every time, there is little point in having lots of close catching fielders.

...when using weak bowlers

If a relatively poor bowler must bowl for any reason, the best tactic is often to limit the potential damage by containing the free scoring of runs.

Off and Leg Side Fields

Another consideration when setting a field is how many fielders to have on each side of the pitch. With nine fielders to place, the division must necessarily be unequal, but the degree of inequality varies.

When describing a field setting, the numbers of fielders on the off side and leg side are often abbreviated into a shortened form, with the off side number quoted first. For example, a 5-4 field means 5 fielders on the off side and 4 on the leg side.

Usually, most fielders are placed on the off side. This is because most bowlers tend to concentrate the line of their deliveries on or outside the off stump, so most shots are hit into the off side.

When attacking, there may be 3 or 4 slips and 1 or 2 gullies, potentially using up to six fielders in that region alone. This would typically be accompanied by a mid off, mid on, and fine leg, making it a 7-2 field. Although there are only two fielders on the leg side, they should get relatively little work as long as the bowlers maintain a line outside off stump. This type of field leaves large gaps in front of the wicket, and is used to entice the batsmen to attack there, with the hope that they make a misjudgment and edge the ball to the catchers waiting behind them.

As fields get progressively more defensive, fielders will move out of the slip and gully area to cover more of the field, leading to 6-3 and 5-4 fields.

If a bowler, usually a leg spin bowler, decides to attack the batsman's legs in an attempt to force a stumping, bowl him behind his legs, or induce a catch on the leg side, the field may stack 4-5 towards the leg side. It is unusual to see more than 5 fielders on the leg side, because of the restriction that there must be no more than two fielders placed behind square leg.

Leg Theory

Sometimes a spinner will bowl leg theory and have seven fielders on the leg side, and will bowl significantly wide of the leg stump to prevent scoring. Often the ball is so wide that the batsman cannot hit the ball straight of mid-on while standing still, and cannot hit to the off side unless they try unorthodox and risky shots such as a reverse sweep or pull, or switch their handedness. The batsman can back away to the leg side to hit through the off side, but can expose their stumps in doing so.

Off Theory

The reverse tactic can be used, by fast and slow bowlers alike, by placing seven or eight fielders on the off side and bowling far outside off stump. The batsman can safely allow the ball to pass without fear of it hitting the stumps, but will not score. If they want to score they will have to try and risk an edge to a wide ball and hit through the packed off side, or trying and drag the ball from far outside the stumps to the sparsely-populated leg side.

Another attacking placement on the leg side is the leg side trap, which involves placing fielders near the boundary at deep square and backward square leg and bowling bouncers to try to induce the batsman to hook the ball into the air. For slower bowlers, the leg trap fieldsmen tend to be placed within 10–15 m from the bat behind square, to catch leg glances and sweeps.

The names of cricket fielding positions can be baffling to the uninitiated. It takes a little while before such names as fine leg, gully or third man become second nature. However, fielding is such a vital part of the game that all players need to be familiar with these strange terms. And, once you know them, listening to the radio commentary takes on another dimension.

The fielders are placed by the captain, depending on his tactics. This is a challenge in itself, because out of the eleven players on the field, one must bowl and another must keep wicket. The nine remaining fielders are simply too few to defend all parts of a cricket field, so their deployment depends on the captain's skill and the bowler's accuracy. No captain can set cricket fielding positions for bad bowling. However, a bowler who "bowls to his field" can pressurise batsmen, and pressure leads to falling wickets.

In days gone by, fielding was regarded as a chore in between batting and bowling. Now, fielding skills are a vital part of the game, and can make the difference between winning and losing a match. Once the fielders can treat every ball as a big event, they are on their way to winning the game.

This picture shows the "standard" cricket fielding positions for a right handed batsman. They are a mirror image for left handers. However, the positions can be varied almost infinitely, depending on tactics.

If a position is described as "deep" or "long", then the fielder is usually placed on the boundary, eg deep mid off. A position labelled as "short" is usually closer to the batsman than normal, eg short cover. And a position prefixed by "silly" is very close to the batsman, eg silly mid off.

Other variations use the terms “square” and “fine”. The line of sight from a square fielder is at right angles to the wicket, eg square leg, or square cover. Conversely, the line of sight from a “fine” fielder is more parallel to the wicket, eg fine third man.

Many players are expert in particular cricket fielding positions. Specialist slip fielders have the fast reactions and acrobatic agility to take catches that can come quickly and at all angles. Expert cover fielders have the speed and agility to cut off potential boundary shots, and to throw the ball fast and accurately over the stumps to the wicketkeeper. Deep fielders have good judgement for high catches, and a strong throwing arm to return the ball quickly and prevent runs.

The wicketkeeper has special skills that are unique within any cricket team. He stands behind the wickets, and catches all balls that pass the batsman – off the bat or otherwise. The faster the bowler, the further back from the wickets he will stand. However, for slow bowlers, the wicket keeper will stand close to the wickets to try and dismiss the batsman by stumping. The wicketkeeper is also well placed to tell the captain about any potential weaknesses shown by the batsman

The slip fielders stand next to the wicket keeper. Their objective is to take catches that fly off the edge of the bat. The slips need to have fast reactions and often, acrobatic agility to take difficult, fast moving catches, or simply to cut off potential edges to the boundary. First slip is often set deeper than the wicketkeeper, because fine edges can travel very quickly indeed.

Third man is usually viewed as a defensive cricket fielding position, to prevent anything passing the slips or gully from reaching the boundary. Third man is usually responsible for covering a large area. However, some bowlers place a short third man to prevent singles, or even take catches that fly past the gully.

Gully must field shots that are often hit hard off the face of the bat. So, this is another specialist position that needs fast reactions and a safe pair of hands, to stop runs and take spectacular catches.

Point is a very busy position, where the fielder must be prepared to field hard hit square cuts or drives off the

face of the bat. Or, a slow bowler may place this fielder at "silly point" – very close to the batsman, to catch any bat/pad chances.

Any fielder in a **"silly" position** may have to take rapid evasive action to avoid any hard hit shots. ECB regulations also prevent junior fielders from standing less than 11 or 8 metres from the bat, depending on age. And, regardless of age, anyone fielding very close to the bat should wear a protective helmet and shin guards.

The **cover position** includes the area between point and mid off. It's another key position for putting pressure on batsmen by cutting off runs and threatening run-outs. Many of the world's outstanding fielders have fielded at point and cover.

Mid off is a key cricket fielding position for cutting off straight drives and stopping quick singles. It is also a good position for the captain to field, so that he can discuss tactics with the bowler – or simply offer encouragement when things are not going according to plan.

Mid wicket and square leg are generally defensive positions for cutting off boundaries and preventing quick singles. However, they must also be prepared for sharp catches that may come their way from misjudged hooks and pulls.

Fine leg is often treated by captains as the best cricket fielding position to rest his bowlers between overs, or after a long bowling spell. However, it can still be a busy area if batsmen are skilled at playing the ball square or fine off their legs. As with any deep position, it can be difficult to pick up the flight or line of the ball coming toward you, so make sure that you've picked these up before you move too far – to avoid embarrassment!

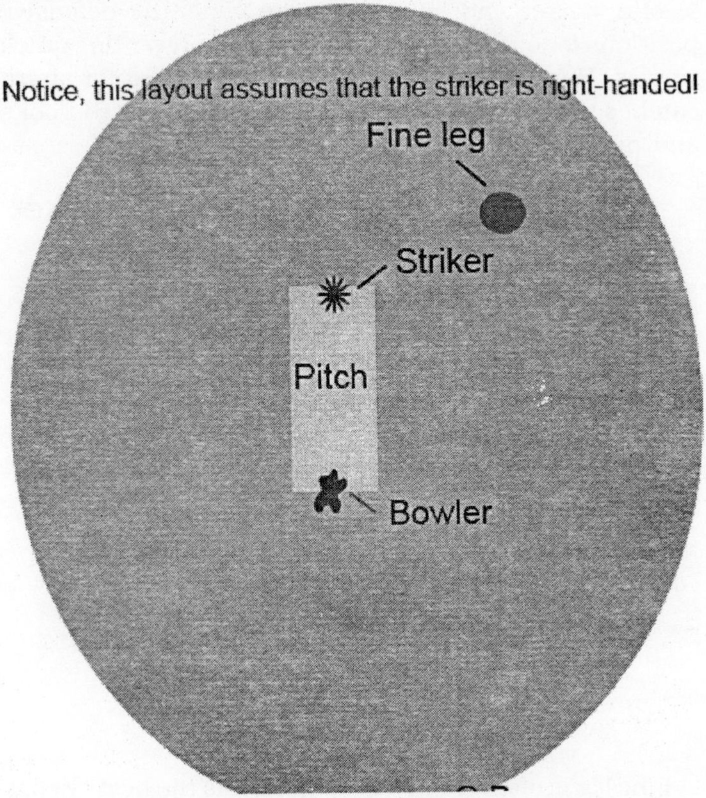

Notice, this layout assumes that the striker is right-handed!

Fine leg

Striker

Pitch

Bowler

3

FIELDING EQUIPMENT

No member of the fielding side other than the wicket-keeper may wear gloves or external leg guards, though fielders (in particular players fielding near to the bat) may also wear shin protectors, groin protectors ('boxes') and chest protectors beneath their clothing. Apart from the wicket-keeper, protection for the hand or fingers may be worn only with the consent of the umpires.

Fielders are permitted to wear a helmet and face guard. This is usually employed in a position such as

silly point or silly mid-wicket, where proximity to the batsman gives little time to avoid a shot directly at their head. Due to the discomfort, the duty of fielding "under the helmet" or "under the lid" is often delegated to the most junior member of the team. If the helmet is only being used for overs from one end, it will be placed behind the wicketkeeper when not in use. Some grounds have purpose-built temporary storage in the form of a cavity beneath the pitch, approximately 1m × 1m × 1m in size, accessed through a hatch flush with the grass, which can be used for storing a helmet, shin pads or drinks for the fielding side. 5 penalty runs are awarded to the batting side should the ball touch a fielder's headgear whilst it is not being worn unless the ball previously struck a batsman not attempting to hit or

avoid the ball. This rule was introduced in the 19th century to prevent the unfair practice of a fielder using a hat (often a top hat) to take a catch.

As cricket balls are hard and can travel at high speeds off the bat, protective equipment is recommended to prevent injury. There have been some recorded deaths in cricket, but they are rare.

4

FIELDING TECHNIQUES

Cricket is team sport which consisted of 12 players in both teams. Out of 12 players, only 11 players used to play with one player kept reserved for substitution.

Out of the 11 players on the field, one player act as a wicketkeeper, one player resume the position of a bowler, the remaining players keep the position of the different positions on the field as imparted by the team captain according to the bowler.

The field placings used to change over usually after the interval and beginning of a new over depending upon the bowler's tactics and the situation around. The team captain is the ultimate authority and each team member have to follow the directions and orders of the captain; it is the captain's decision to either go for defensive or attacking outfields depending upon the situation of the match.

The following are some fielding positions on which the fielders used to field on the cricket ground on the captain's signal and according to the bowler's bowling tactics :

I. OUT-FIELD

1. Long-Off
2. Long-On
3. Deep Mid-Off

4. Deep Extra
5. Extra Cover
6. Deep Point
7. Deep Third Main
8. Third Man
9. Deep Fine Leg
10. Long Leg
11. Deep Square Leg
12. Deep Mid Wicket
13. Deep Mid On

II. IN-FIELD

1. Mid-off
2. Mid-on
3. Mid Wicket
4. Short Extra Cover
5. Cover Point
6. Backward Point
7. Point
8. Gully
9. Short Third Man
10. Short Fine Leg
11. Backward Square Leg
12. Square Leg

III. CLOSE-IN-FIELD

1. First Slip
2. Second Slip
3. Third Slip
4. Fourth Slip
5. Silly Point
6. Silly Mid-off
7. Short Mid-off
8. Short Mid-on
9. Silly Mid-on
10. Forward Short Leg
11. Backward Short Leg
12. Leg Slip

I. OUT-FIELD

This is the outermost zone of the cricket field consisted of about thirteen (13) fielding positions which are as follows :

1. Long-Off

This is the important position located at the outfield. The area situated at the offside of the batsman's position near the boundary. Usually, players having good height used to field there because there are chances of batsman out by catch the ball.

2. Long-On

This is the important position located at the outfield.

Playing field and playing positions

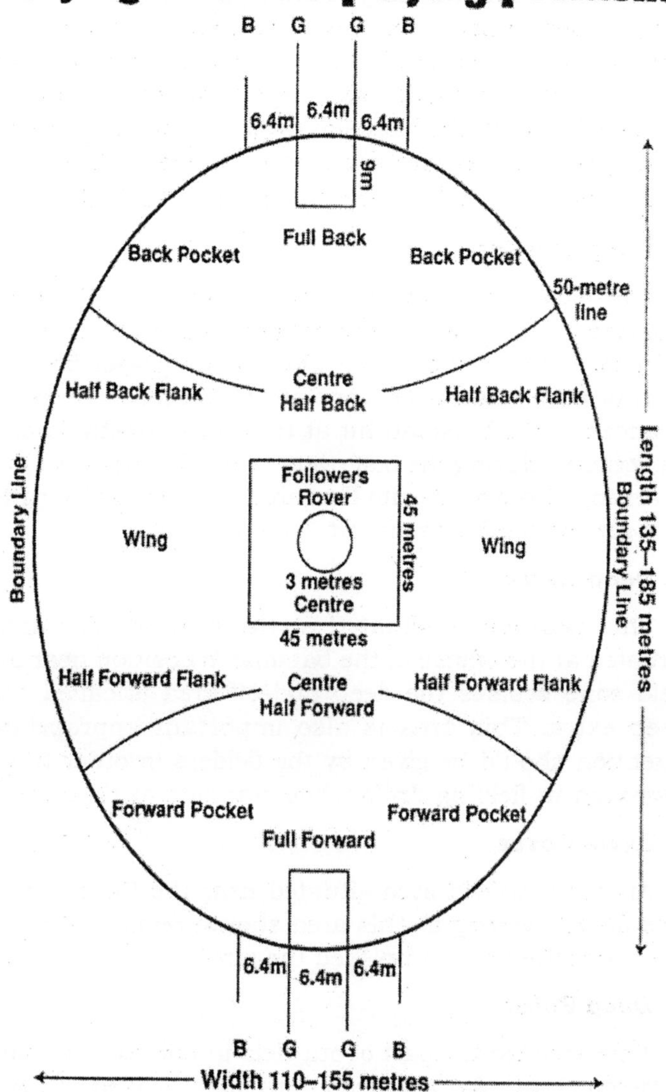

The area situated at the legside of the batsman's position near the boundary. Usually, players having good height used to field there because there are chances of batsman out by catch the ball. In one day cricket, this position becomes particularly important because during the last 10 overs, the batsmen used to score big runs by hitting boundaries and sixes and one loose stroke will cause their wicket by catch by the long-on fielder.

3. Deep Mid-Off

This position is situated at the outfield. The area situated at the offside of the batsman's position near in-field zone is known as Deep Mid-Off. The player fielding at this area should be very alert as there are great chances of the batsman hit at that area. Mostly in one day cricket, during the last overs to go, the captain used to arrange his players into that area in order to stop runs and getting the batsman out.

4. Deep Extra

This position is situated at the outfield. The area situated at the offside of the batsman's position near in-field zone besides the deep mid-off area is called the deep extra. This area is also important appropriate attention should be given by the fielders in order to be thorough in fielding drills while standing at this area.

5. Extra Cover

Another outfield area situated near the Deep Extra. The fielder fielding at this area should remain alert all the times the batsman played the stroke.

6. Deep Point

This area too the part of out-field in cricket. The zone between extra cover and deep third man is called as Deep

Point. The fielder positioned at this area should be very keen to hold the ball coming towards him.

7. Deep Third Man

The area near third man and next to Deep Point is called as Deep Third Man. The fielder fielding at this area should have athletic flexibility in order to move to hold the ball passing by him to save the runs.

8. Third Man

This area also comes under out-field. Third Man is an important fielding position situated before Deep Third Man. Usually, captain employed only one fielder at Deep Third Man or Third Man in order to stop runs or catching position.

9. Deep Fine Leg

Deep Fine Leg is also out-field position. It is situated before short fine leg area. Very rarely captain employed his fielders at this area depending upon the circumstances of the match.

10. Long Leg

An outfield area just parallel to short fine leg. This area is very important because mostly batsmen used to sweep the spin bowlers at this area in order to get a boundary or sixes. The fielder fielding at this area should be very keen to hold the ball.

11. Deep Square Leg

It is another important outfield area which is situated before square leg. Generally leg umpire used to stand besides this area watching the situation from leg side. The batsman strong in leg side used to play stroke at this area in order to score runs in the form of boundaries and sixes, so the fielder fielding at this area should be very alert and always keep his eyes on the ball coming towards him.

12. Deep Mid Wicket

It is yet another outfield zone which is situated before mid-wicket. The fielder positioned at this area should be perfect in fielding skills viz., throwing, and specially taking catches as there are great chances of batsman play the loose stroke in the air in his effort to score boundaries and sixes.

13. Deep Mid-On

It is another outfield area which is situated between deep mid wicket and long-on zone. The fielder fielding at this particular area should have athletic flexibilities as the batsmen used to play their authentic strokes to this area in order to get runs.

II. IN-FIELD

This is another important fielding zone situated just next to out-field zone. There are about twelve (12) fielding positions in in-field zone. Each positions have their relevant place in fielding. Some of the in-field positions are cover point, mid-wicket, square leg etc., and those who are positioned in similar positions specially in the one day cricket matches who used to field at the edge of the 30 yard circle are the quickest and very often a team's best fielders. The in-field fielders should have the appropriate agilities viz., one-handed pick-up at speed, combined with early and accurate throwing abilities etc. The following are the brief discussions pertaining these twelve (12) fielding positions :

1. Mid-Off

This is an important position in every class of cricket, because it is such a good place for a captain to field. From mid-off, the captain can so easily advise and encourage the bowler. His exact position will vary slightly according to the batsman and the bowler; thus for a defensive batsman, mid-off can move up to within about 18 yards of the bat, but for a strong attacking batsman he is usually 25 to 30 yards away. His main job is to stop and hold all the off-drives within his reach.

Many balls which are well pitched up and in the vicinity of the off stump will be hit hard and firmly along the ground in mid-off's direction. If these are mistimed slightly, a possible catch will often result, but it is likely to be a hard catch, hard in the sense that the ball will be travelling fast rather than one requiring acrobatic ability to reach and hold it.

Many mid-offs are solidly built fellows with large tough hands. Yet they cannot afford to be solid and inactive because they must be ready to dash in a counter the semi-defensive push stroke which sends the ball slowly in their direction and gives the batsman a quick run if mid-off is a slow starter.

2. Mid-On

One of the few places on the cricket field where it is possible to hid a poor fielder is mid-on. Like his counterpart, mid-off, the exact position he occupies will vary according to circumstances, but unlike mid-off, he will have far fewer drives to stop or catches to hold. The reason is simply that it is easier for a batsman to drive a ball on the off-side, the bad balls outside the leg stump being generally placed more squarely in the direction of the umpire or mid-wicket.

3. Mid-Wicket

It is important in-field zone which is situated between silly mid-on and deep mid-wicket. A good fielder should be employed at this fielding position as there are great chances of batsman to play his relevant stroke at this area.

4. Short Extra

It is import in-field positions situated besides the cover point. Usually batsman hit the ball to this position in order to get single run, so the fielder should keep himself very alert all the times on the field and specially when the batsman is about to play the ball.

5. Cover Point

Probably more run-outs result from the cover point position than from any other part of the field. The distance the cover fieldsman in that position should be the quickest mover and the most accurate short distance thrower in the team. He must learn to anticipate each stroke by watching the direction of each delivery and the movements of the batsman's feet. If he plays forward to a ball well pitched up, he should not move in too quickly as a hard hit at cover may easily beat the fieldsman.

If he plays back, then he should move in quickly to prevent a possible short single, as the ball is less likely to be hit hard in back play. A ball driven to cover seldom maintains a straight line but usually spins away in a direction to the left of the fieldsman if driven by the right handed batsman.

The other specialist fielding positions are near the batsman, i.e., silly-mid-off, silly-mid-on, short square leg and short fine leg. These fielders have got to be alert all the time and above all they have got to be courageous, active and sure catchers. They should not try to move away the head when the batsman is about to swing his bat. They should keep an eye on the bat until the batsman has played the ball.

6. Backward Point

An in-field zone situated between the cover point and point. The fielder fielding at this position should be very alert as there are wide scope of runs scored by the batsman by hitting the ball towards this position. Usually, a fielder having perfect in fielding drills should be placed at this location.

7. Point

Another in-field position situated between the backward point and short third-man next to gully. The fielder fielding at this area should be well versed in fielding skills and should have abilities to pick-up and throw the ball at speed by one-hand to the appropriate destination.

8. Gully

It is an important in-field position in cricket. The fielder positioning at this position should have athletic flexibilities as there always the possibilities of ball coming to this end as the batsman in order to hit the off-stump ball to the fence to score runs.

9. Short Third-Man

Speed round the boundary edge, ability to pick up on the run and accurate long-distance, throwing are the main requisites for third man. Catches are comparatively rare in this position, but, as third man often goes to long field at the end of the over, it is a mistake to imagine that he need not be a good catcher, for it is obviously impossible for any player to field at third man at both ends.

As a general principle, his chief task is to save the two, a cut or sliced drive in his direction will usually be a certain run, and it will become two runs if he hesitates before returning the ball to the wicket-keeper. Mentally, it is an easy position, because there is no need for great concentration on every ball.

10. Short Fine Leg

It is yet another in-field position which is situated between the short third-man and backward square leg. Usually, very rare strokes are played by the batsman at this end and hence, the poor fielders may also positioned at this end.

11. Backward Square Leg

This fielding position is situated next to leg slip area. It is an important fielding position and fielder appointed there should be very alert and have fielding efficiency skills as there are great chances of batsman hitting at this end.

12. Square Leg

Square leg is yet position at in-field area which

requires appropriate attentions and efficient fielding skills as the batsman who is strong in playing leg side strokes used to hit the ball at this end.

III. CLOSE-INFIELD

This is a most important fielding zone situated just next to in-field zone. There are about twelve (12) fielding positions in close-infield zone. Each positions have their relevant place in fielding. The fielders of close-infield usually are the team's best and specialist fielders having fielding skills including one-hand throw at speed, with accurate follow through. Some of the important fielding positions in close-infield are forward short leg, silly point, silly mid-on, silly mid-off etc. The general aspects and outlook of the close-infield remains the same in today's cricket with the growing numbers of protective covering and equipments and facilities for the fielders who are fielding at the suicidal positions at close-infield.

The following are the brief discussions pertaining these twelve (12) close-infield positions :

1. First Slip

According to the type of bowler and the condition of the pitch, there may be one, two, three or even, very occasionally, four slips. Comparative immobility of foot, extraordinary quickness of eye, arms, hands, and fingers and intense concentration are the main attributes of a first class slip fielders.

The slip fielders should take up their positions where they feel ball will come to them at a convenient height if it is snicked by the batsman. Their feet should be spaced comfortably apart for balance, but not so far apart to prevent them springing sideways immediately off either foot.

Knees should be slightly bent with the body bent over to suit the height of the fieldsman. Hands should be kept easily in front of the body with the fingers relaxed and pointing slightly downwards.

The whole body should be slightly relaxed and ready for quick movement in any direction.

First slip should stand sufficiently wide of the wicket-keeper so that his vision will not be obstructed when the keeper has to move across to take a ball on the off side. Other slip fielders should be so placed that a ball played between them may be reached by either without colliding with the other.

2. Second Slip

The second slip fielder should be stand sufficiently wide of the first slip fielder so that his vision will not be obstructed by the first slip fielder. The fielder should stand in a position which suit his eye level and where he may better judge the ball edged from the batsman's bat.

3. Third Slip

The third slip fielder should be positioned sufficiently wide from the second fielder so that there may be less chances of the obstruction and collision among the slip fielders. Again, the third slip fielder should stand at the position away from the second slip fielder and from where he may judge the ball coming towards him.

4. Fourth Slip

The fourth slip fielder should take his positioned away

from the third slip fielder. There should be enough gap between the third and fourth slip fielders as there always the chances of collision between the slip fielders while holding the ball or taking catch.

All slip fielders should be on the alert for a rebound from the keeper or from the hands of adjacent fieldsmen, and should be prepared to back up the keeper and attend the wicket if the latter happens to rush away to recover a ball which has been played a short distance away from the wicket.

5. Silly Point

This is one of the important close-infield position which is also called as suicidal position as there always be a danger of batsman playing the strokes towards the fielder positioned at the silly point area. But nowadays in modern cricket, with the amendment and advancement in the protective equipments and facilities for the fielders, there are less chances of fielders get hurt. The team's specialist fielders used to take this position depending upon the circumstances of the match.

6. Silly Mid-off

It is another close-infield position situated next to silly point. This area is very crucial and important from fielder's point of view. The batsman used to play at this end in order to get singles and play for long drive towards the silly mid-off fielder so the person appointed at this end should keep himself alert and should always keep his eyes on the ball coming towards him.

7. Short Mid-off

It is also as important as other close-infield positions

such as silly point, silly mid-off etc., because the batsmen used to hit the ball in order to get single at this end. Usually, team's specialist and best fielders should be appointed at this end.

8. Short Mid-on

This position is very much appropriate to the team's captain leading the fielding team as the captain may provide his necessary advises and suggestions to the bowler and discuss with him the necessary precautions and match strategies.

9. Silly Mid-on

This location is situated between forward short leg and short mid on. Again team's best fielders usually appointed at this end as there always be the chances of the ball coming towards this end by the batsman in order to score run. The fielder fielding at this end should be very alert and should have athletic activities and flexibilities in order to hold the ball and take some extraordinary catches which may change the match outlook.

10. Forward Short-Leg

This is another important close-infield area which is situated next to silly mid-on. This is the most suicidal position in the cricket field as the fielder has to stand nearby the batsman who may play some attacking strokes which may hurt the fielders positioned at the forward short-leg area. In today's cricket with the advancement of the protective equipments and facilities, there are now less chances of the fielders get hurted as the fielder used to field there by wearing a safety helmet on the head but still this is an crucial and suicidal position in the cricket field.

11. Backward Short-Leg

It is situated near and next to forward short-leg area. Usually team's best and specialist fielder used to field at this end as the ball soundly hit by the batsman with full momentum used to pass by the fielder standing there. So, the fielders should be positioned there with wearing safety covering to avoid injuries. This is another suicidal position in the cricket field.

12. Leg Slip

It is yet another close-infield position which is situated near and besides the backward short-leg behind the wicketkeeper. The fielder having less and poor fielding efficiency may be placed at this end as the ball barely pass through this end.

5

WICKETKEEPING

The wicket-keeper in the sport of cricket is the player on the fielding side who stands behind the wicket or stumps being guarded by the batsman currently on strike. The wicket-keeper is the only member of the fielding side permitted to wear gloves and external leg guards. The wicket-keeper may also wear a helmet with a mesh face guard to help protect from injury.

It is essentially a specialist role although a keeper is occasionally called upon to bowl, in which case another member of the fielding side temporarily keeps wicket. The role of the keeper is governed by Law 40 of the Laws of Cricket.

Purposes

The keeper's major function is to stop deliveries that pass the batsman (in order to prevent runs being scored as 'byes'), but he can also attempt to dismiss the batsman in various ways:

The most common dismissal effected by the keeper is for him to catch a ball that has nicked the batsman's bat, called an edge, before it bounces. Sometimes the keeper is also in the best position to catch a ball which has been hit high in the air. More catches are taken by wicket-keepers than by any other fielding position.

The keeper can stump the batsman by using the ball to remove the bails from the stumps, if the batsman has come out of his crease during a delivery.

When the ball is hit into the outfield, the keeper moves close to the stumps to catch the return throw from a fielder and, if possible, to run out a batsman.

A keeper's position depends on the bowler: for fast

bowling he will crouch some distance from the stumps, in order to have time to react to edges from the batsman, while for slower bowling, he will come much nearer to the stumps (known as "standing up"), to pressure the batsman into remaining within the crease or risk being stumped. The more skilled the keeper, the faster the bowling to which he is able to "stand up", for instance Godfrey Evans often stood up to Alec Bedser.

Wicket-keeping is a specialist discipline and it requires training consistent with the level expected of a specialist batsman or bowler. However, the modern-day

keeper is also expected to possess reasonable batting skill, suiting him for the middle order at least. Wicket-keepers who are also capable of batting at the top of the order are known informally as keeper/batsmen.

Since there is only room for one keeper in a cricket side, selectors (especially at the international level) are often faced with a difficult choice between two or more skilled keepers. Often, one of the two keepers is an exceptional keeper, but only an average batsman, whereas the other is a keeper/batsman who is clearly better at batting, but not quite as good a keeper as his rival. One such selection dilemma was that faced by England selectors in the 1990s between Jack Russell (the pure keeper) and Alec Stewart (the keeper/batsman). They were never able to consistently choose between the two until 1998, when Russell began to fade: prior to that, they had regularly swapped the role, often with Stewart maintaining his place when not wicket-keeping thanks to his batting skill. Another prime example is that of Pakistani wicketkeeper Kamran Akmal, who is renowned for being a very inconsistent wicketkeeper who fluffs easy chances, but has remained a fixture in the team over the last decade because his batting is considerably superior to the alternatives'. Mahendra Singh Dhoni, Kumar Sangakkara, Matt Prior and Brendon McCullum are the top keeper/batsmen today in cricket.

The keeper may also have a captaincy role. Uniquely, they are usually involved in every delivery of an innings, and may be in a position to see things that the captain misses. They can frequently be heard encouraging the bowler, and may also indulge in the practice (not meant to be overheard) of "sledging" the batsman with well timed comments about their skill, appearance or personal habits.

The keeper is the only fielder allowed to touch the ball with protective equipment, typically large padded gloves with webbing between the index finger and thumb, but no other webbing. The protection offered by the gloves is not always adequate. The England keeper Alan Knott sometimes placed steaks inside his gloves for added cushioning. Wicket-keepers also tend to wear leg pads and a box to protect the groin area.

Wicket-keepers are allowed to take off their pads and bowl, though this rarely happens but is not uncommon when matches are drifting to draws or a bowling team is desperate for a wicket. Two keepers have removed their pads and taken hat-tricks in first-class cricket: Probir Sen for Bengal v Orissa at Cuttack in 1954–55 and A.C. (Alan) Smith for Warwickshire v Essex at Clacton in 1965; Smith was a most unusual player in that he was primarily a wicket-keeper, but was sometimes selected as a frontline bowler.

Wicket keeping is an exciting and exacting aspect of game of cricket. It can be said that a cricket team is never complete without a wicket keeper. Importance of wicket keeper can be measured from the fact that wicket keeper is the pivot of fielding side. In all the actions related to all the deliveries, wicket keeper get involved. It can be said that role of wicket keeper in the game of cricket is very crucial and for this, wicket keeper has to keep a keen watch on all the balls delivered.

As we know that captain is one of an important player or part of a cricket team and various kinds of questions are being run in his mind on the ground. To get the answers of various kinds of questions, captain consults the wicket keeper from time to time.

The importance of wicket-keeping is emphasised by the fact that whilst there are 11 players to bat and several to bowl in a team, there is only one to keep wickets. On him falls the entire responsibility of accepting fine snicks and effecting stumpings and run-cuts as well as keeping byes down to a minimum. While he is on the field, it is a whole time job, one for a true specialist. It is only possible for a player to become a good wicket keeper if he practise hard and applied correct techniques.

PRINCIPLES OF WICKET KEEPING

While proficiency only comes as the result of practice and experience, there are a few fundamental rules for good wicket-keeping which you will see obeyed by almost all first-class players; here are some of them:

-Take every possible ball with two hands, with the fingers pointing downwards and never towards the direction of the approaching ball. When the ball arrives higher than the top of the stumps, the elbows have to be bent in order to raise the height of the wrists and thus allow the hands to assume the downward position. When the ball comes as far up as your face, you should point the right hand out towards the off side and at the same time bring the left hand up underneath it.

-Never snatch at the ball; just allow it to come into the open cup made by your two hands, which then close round the ball. Allow the hands to 'give' just a few inches, bending back slightly at the wrists.

-Keep your feet as firm as possible; try to avoid moving either, but if necessary move only one, the right one for balls wide of the off stump and the left for balls on the leg side.

-Stand as close as possible to the wicket—'nose on the bails' is a well-known slogan—except when the pace makes it advisable to stand back; in that case, stand right back, so as to take the ball on the long hop.

By following all the above mentioned principles, one can become an outstanding wicket keeper without getting any kind of injuries.

HOW TO PREPARE FOR THE MATCH

On match morning, rise early to give yourself ample time for preparation and the journey to the ground. Your first aim should be to do loosening and stretching exercises for between fifteen and thirty minutes. Be on the cricket ground at least an hour before play. Do a few more loosening and stretching exercises to offset possible a long drive in the car. An hour's ride or more can stiffen the backs of the legs and since the hamstring and calf muscles are so important in a wicket keeper's job, it is wise to look after them.

Loosening Up

After a few exercises, trot round the ground to prepare your legs for the running they will have to do in the field and running will do if you are batting.

Nerves

Nerves, dry the mouth and when the five minute bell goes, pop in a piece of chewing gum. Do not constantly run and jump with the gum in your mouth, and as soon as the dryness has done, remove it. The problem is then where to put it. Spectators have possibly seen you in an odd moment stalking about the end of the square like a gold prospector. The probability is that you are seeking a suitable burial ground for the spent gum which sometimes finds its last resting place in an old stump hole.

Once the captain says, right lads, let us go, a keeper should realize that he is a key man. His skill will give bowlers confidence for he has far more chance in helping to dismiss a batsman than any other fielder. Not the least important part of a wicket keeper's work is in taking returns. Agility and anticipation can make even the bad throw look good. So do not just stand at the stumps and let a wild throw go flashed by. Move and set everyone an example. Be ready also to advise your skipper, if he approaches you on any situation or problem, for you are in a position to assess the strengths and weaknesses of a particular batsman and the nature of the wicket.

WICKETKEEPING SKILLS AND TECHNIQUES

STANCE

Just as a batsman has to have a stance, so too does the wicket keeper. Stances vary but one essential point to remember is comfort. It is no good copying someone else and then finding that their position imposes a strain. Bending the knees fully helps to relax the back which otherwise might curve a great deal. The next thing to study is balance with the weight evenly distributed between your feet so that you are ready to move in any direction, but the most important factor is sighting the ball.

In the stance position, you should look at the ball with your eyes level. To tilt the head on one side or turn it slightly means that you are trying to sight the ball

unnaturally. Another point is blinking. Some people have higher blinking rates than others, but when you are keeping you must make sure you never blink once the ball is on its way to you. In that fraction of a second that your eyes are closed, the ball might deviate and the necessary re-sighting could lose you the chance of a dismissal.

It is found that while waiting for the ball to be delivered, some keepers place their hands on the ground between their legs. Others rest them on their knees. There are a few who have their fingers resting on the ground outside their legs. This is very comfortable, but it is found when standing up that sometimes it is a little late in bringing keeper's hands together. So, if you use this stance, make sure your hands are ready work as a unit in taking.

Thus The wicket-keeper's stance should be such that he is comfortable and there is no strain, with the help of which he can get the best possible view of bowler right from the time he takes a start and delivers the ball, that the ball is collected with the minimum of movement, that he is so close to the wicket that after taking the ball, he can comfortably break the wicket.

STANDING BACK

A wicket-keeper must stand either right up or right back. He has to stand back to any bowling above medium-pace or to medium-paced bowling on very fast or sticky wickets. By standing in this position, it is easy for him to take catches either on the off or leg side off faster kicking deliveries. In general, he will aim at so positioning himself that the good length ball will reach him just after it starts to drop in its trajectory after pitching.

The first problem to settle when you are standing back is how far you go. Remember the aim should be to catch the ball just after it begins to drop in its trajectory towards you after pitching. Most keepers like to catch at about waist height when standing back, but it is preferred to take the ball at knee height, which means that you can stand an extra yard to so deeper and have that much more time to sight and move after the ball. This can be vital, especially when going for the wide deflections. During the first few overs with the new ball, keeper has to judge the pace and bounce of the wicket, remembering also that the bowlers may be slightly below their full pace until they have completely loosened up.

For the first over or some, stand a little closer than you normally stand because if an edge comes, it is better to be too near than too far away. The deflection can come to you very quickly and at an awkward height, but atleast you have a chance which is denied to you if the ball bounces well before reaching your gloves. Before the ball is bowled, scrape the ground with your hands which will give you a standing mark. This is just a guide which you can change, once the bowlers are delivering at their full pace.

While standing back in the stance position, place yourself wide of the off stump, so that you have a better chance of seeing a good-length ball pitch on the leg or middle stumps. If you stand directly behind the line of the stumps, you will not see those deliveries pitch because they will be hidden by the batsman's body or bat. To take up your position, move across so that when you are squatting, you can see all three stumps at the other end and then go approximately twelve inches wider, so that you can see a gap between the two sets of stumps.

As a general guide, the nearer you are to the stumps when standing back, the smaller this gap will have to be. The closer you are to the batsman, the easier it is to see round his body. The importance of seeing these good length deliveries pitching on leg or middle stump is that they might swing late or seam out towards the off side. In both cases, the ball could pass the off stump with you setting off down the leg side. Some people feel that the difficult work is only done when standing up, and it has been said that when a keeper is standing back, he is terribly wrong. The ball even after pitching, can do all sorts of things. It can swing either way, dip or even rise on its way to your gloves. Those movements can be very late, and this means that you have to watch the ball all the way into your gloves.

Sometimes the ball only swings after it pitches. The absence of swing through the air is caused by the seam of the ball being slightly out of position as it leaves the bowler's hand, but impact with the pitch adjusts it to the correct position with the result that the ball swings on its loop towards you. The ball coming straight through can often bounce towards you at chest height. For a right-handed batsman, with the ball bouncing high and beating or getting a faint outside edge, move to your left slightly inside the line of the ball turning your shoulder to the right taking it to the right of your chest. If you move to your right and the edge is a little thicker than you have judged, then you still have the problem of the chest height catch with the ball following you. Another way to take such awkward deliveries is to bend the knees slightly so that the ball comes at you neck or head level, catching it with the fingers pointing up.

SQUATTING

Squat with your hands placed on the ground between your legs, and when you are down, always keep on your toes. This is not because it is necessary the right thing to do, but because it is comfortable for you. When you have tried squatting with your heels on the ground, you have to struggle to prevent yourself from falling backwards.

When you are squatting on your toes, your weight should be always slightly forward and you should feel more ready to move off quickly. As the bowler comes in, sway or rock gently from side to side, giving you the feeling that you are ready to move off in either direction, but you are very careful not to move your head.

Thus for all the wicket keepers, squatting position is recommended, with the seat very close to the ground and the weight evenly distributed as well as balanced between both feet. The back of the hands will initially be resting on the ground between the legs. The

advantage of this position is that it minimizes muscular strain and provides the best possible sight of the ball. The left foot is behind the middle and off stumps and the right will be parallel with it some distance away. Both feet will directly be pointing down the pitch. The body and head must be kept still, and it is of vital importance that they stay down as long as possible, only rising to meet the rise of the ball off the pitch.

CATCHING THE BALL

As said earlier that a wicket keeper have to catch all the deliveries if the ball is coming near the stumps. Because the direction in which the ball will come is not certain, wicket keeper have to stretch or move his body around the wicket from time to time. There are various manners in which a wicket keeper can catch the ball, some of which have been discussed in this chapter.

Diving Catch : No greater thrill exists for wicket keeper than to take off, stretching every inch of leg, body and arms to claw a wide deflection into your eager gloves. For off-side edges that are thicker and so deviate away from you, you must move as quickly as you can and dive if necessary. Strong and supple legs are needed to lift you from your squatting position to move before launching and making your attempt to catch. It is very rare in first class cricket to see a keeper go for a two-handed diving catch in the same way as a goalkeeper goes down to save a shot.

A goalkeeper can afford to ground the ball, but a wicket keeper must keep the ball off the turf at all costs, so he forms his catching cup, the one we use most, with the little finger of each hand meeting. A much wider span can be achieved by diving to take the ball one-handed. How great this difference is you can judge by standing against a wall with your hands and arms parallel to the ground in front of you. Now ask someone to act as a marker at the point, where your fingertips reach and turn your body 90 degrees to the right or left with one shoulder still against the wall. Stretch out the arm which is not pressed against the ball and you will note that the fingertips are beyond your friend, in fact, the distance gained when going for a one-handed catch is almost the width of your shoulders. A keeper may think he can only reach the ball with one hand, and then, finding it not so wide as he first thought brings his other hand comfortably on top of the ball, as it enters the original glove.

For all diving catches, it is necessary to avoid jarring the hands or forearms. So on taking the ball, try and lift the gloves away from the ground, and land on the side of your body or even on your back. The essential point in taking diving catches is to be natural. Do not either stop your body from rolling over or exaggerate the roll so that you fail to concentrate on the ball.

Wrestlers never stop themselves from rolling after they have been thrown, because they know that resistance to their fall could be dangerous. So let you body do the natural thing. Throw it and if you go with the ball and roll, you are much more likely to hold the catch. Loosening exercises are a tremendous help to wicket keepers in taking diving catches, especially the stretching ones for your shoulders, and arms. Sometimes a keeper will be criticized for diving when the deflection did not seem all that wide of him, but it all depends on the pace and the bounce. If the ball comes through normally, you may have a chance to move your feet and take the catch without diving, but sometimes it skids through quick and low, and you have no time to do more than dive after it.

Diving Catches on Off Side

In taking diving catches on the off side, most keepers are set an unfair problem, you must only dive for those you feel will not carry to first slip. With such a thought in your mind, it is likely that you will often fail to dive for edge which do not reach first slip.

Once the stroke is being made, you have a fraction of

a second in which to make a decision. During any slight hesitation, the chance will probably have gone. A keeper must be allowed to go freely for any catches he thinks he can take, so that there is no hesitation or half-hearted effort.

When a keeper takes a one-handed catch in front of first slip's waist, it reveals that the fielder could be standing too close to him. First slip should be one of the best catchers on the field and athletic enough to dive at full stretch. He should not stand so close to the keeper that he can only dive away from him. When an edge from a right hander is going between the keeper and first slip, the keeper should dive to his right and slip to his left. First slip stands about two feet deeper so that on diving his hands come behind the keeper's hands forming a second line of defence, necessary because standing where he does, slip has a fraction more time to sight the ball.

The distance a keeper can cover depends on the bounce and speed of the delivery and where the ball finds the edge of the bat. If the ball is wide of the off stump and then deflected, the keeper will have already moved across covering its trajectory. In these circumstances, a keeper could take a catch in front of slip. If, however, the ball is edged from off stump, the keeper, being behind the line of it, is that much further from first slip, so when he dives this time he will not reach in front of him.

Inside Edge

The most difficult catch to take standing back is the inside edge which usually occurs when the batsman intends to play a ball out on the off side. Very rarely

does an inside edge chance come when a batsman has intended a shot to leg because part of the body is nearly always behind the line of the delivery. Again the keeper following the line of the ball, is looking for the outside edge when suddenly the ball comes through between the bat and the batsman's pads or body.

Here, the keeper must make a quick change of direction, but he will not be so tested often, because the ball often goes onto the batsman's pads or body, or even hits the stumps. All deliveries bowled down the leg side pass at some time out of the keeper's view, but re-sighting is easier here because the ball generally continues on the line off which it rises from the pitch. If the batsman gets an edge, the ball will go still wider down the leg side and it is here that anticipation can be so vital.

Therefore, always aim to move beyond the original line of the ball as doing this puts you in position for a catch. If the batsman misses the ball and it comes through on its original line, you should still be able to take it comfortably to the right of your body.

Outside Edge

The outside edge catch which is most awkward to take is when the ball pitches on middle, or even leg stump wit the batsman attempting to play to leg but the ball moves late, either in the air or off the pitch. You should try to watch such deliveries pitch, but the difficulty comes when the bowler angles the delivery into the batsman's body and you set of to cover the line of the ball. For an outside edge, in these circumstances, you have both to re-focus and change direction so that the gap between you and first slip has become quite wide. Such chances can prove elusive, though fortunately they are comparatively rare.

Leg-Side Taking

For leg-side deliveries, you must try and see the ball pitch before committing yourself to a movement. If you start off before seeing the ball pitch, you cannot know whether it will bounce high, keep low, or deviate. In fact, you will be gambling on where the ball is coming through. When the ball is pitched right up just outside the batsman's legs, or even further than that, you cannot sight the ball off the pitch, but you will have logged in your mind the right line from its flight and moved your gloves behind it.

Then, you will have to judge what height to hold your hands but with a ball of such full length, the amount of lift should only be very small before reaching your gloves. Such deliveries can be extremely difficult to gather when they land in the rough caused by the bowler's footmarks. Experience in keeping to the different bowlers in your side will be a great help. Study their pace off the wicket and the amount of bounce and movement they achieve off various types of surface. This will help develop your judgement, so that you are in the right position to take the ball cleanly.

While standing up, you should see the ball heading for the leg side you move your left foot slightly towards that side, remembering to keep your head as still as possible so that your eyes are peering round the batsman's body to watch the ball pitch. When you have moved your left foot across, your right follows and then often you need to move your left again, so that you have covered a considerable amount of ground, but your body weight is slightly towards the stumps and the cardinal point is to be able to bring the ball back to the wicket as quickly as possible. You try never to take your right foot so wide of the leg stump that your body is in a position where your hands cannot reach back to the balls.

To bring the ball back to the stumps with two hands means that for all wide deliveries, you must turn your body, especially your shoulders, in to face the stumps so that both arms have the same reach towards the wicket. Being right handed and catching with your little finger placed on top of the little finger of your left hand, you can easily transfer the ball into just your right hand. So, when taking wide deliveries down the leg side to a right hander, and down the off side to a left hander, if you cannot comfortable reach the bails with both hands, you can in the same motion transfer the ball to your right gloves, so that you have the extra reach needed. This method of removing the bails with one hand is a safety device if you happen to be too far away from the line of the stumps, but can also be used as an alternative method of stumping.

Attempting a stumping with the ball in the right glove does not necessarily involve turning your shoulders inwards to face the wicket. You can have them facing down the wicket or even turned slightly away from the stumps, and still reach the bails with your right hand. Taking wide deliveries down the leg side to the left hander or off side to a right hander, you cannot go through the one handed procedure. Transferring the ball to your right hand gains nothing and you find it very awkward and so time wasting to transfer the ball from two hands into just your left.

Left handed keepers can use this one-handed method down the opposite side from the right-hander. It is rather strange, but you can only remember seeing one left handed wicket keeper in first class cricket. It is generally harder to take deliveries when the batsman is playing forward, because the ball is pitched that much closer to you than when he is playing back. But a full half volley is a simpler proposition than a ball pitching two to four feet in front of you.

The half volley can be taken just after it has hit the ground so there is no time for any unusual bounce or change of direction, but the ball pitching shorter, especially if it hits in the rough, has enough space to become unpredictable. The time left for you to detect any unusual movement is so brief that you feel these deliveries are the hardest to take cleanly. A ball well up to the batsman outside his legs has a fair chance of coming through to the keeper.

Behind the Line

For the deliveries coming through just outside the off stump, you should be directly behind the line of the ball. The wider the delivery, say to a right-hand batsman, the wider you will have to move your right foot across trying to make sure that you take it parallel with, or possibly forward but never backwards from, the return crease. This movement brings your head on to, or as near the line of, the ball as possible.

If the stride feels awkward, you should allow your left foot to follow across naturally, so that you are again comfortable and balanced, but be careful not to move your left foot so far that you have difficulty in bringing your hands back to the wicket. Never take your left foot far away from the off stump, because the body weight would then no longer be attacking the wicket, and you cannot reach back comfortable. If the ball is that wide, you should keep your head and body slightly inside the line.

Leg-Side Catch

Another rare catch when standing up is that on the leg side. Most top-class batsmen only drive through mid-on and mid-wicket, or glance when they have part of their pad or body behind the line of the ball so that any misjudgement on their part has much less chance of carrying to hand. There is also the added difficulty of a double deflection from bat and body, which makes the catch extremely hard for a keeper standing up to take, but the most likely leg side chance is when a spinner strays and the batsman sweeps too early or plays this shot too close to his body. In these circumstances, the ball can frequently strike the batsman on the gloves and pop up almost anywhere.

One of the most important questions for wicket-keeper is when to stand up and when to stand back. Twenty years or more ago, keepers used to stand up to the medium and even medium-quick bowlers a great deal more than they do nowadays. Change has been for the better because there is no point in standing up close to the wicket.

Possibly, batsmen played forward far more than they do today, stretching uncomfortably to give stumping chances. Even so, looking back over the records there were not many stumpings off medium pacers. A keeper should not stand up to a medium-paced or medium-quick bowler to save out of bravado. Nor should he do so just for the energy by not having to move and dive for the wide deflections, or sprint to the stumps to take returns. Keepers must be fit to do their job properly. Another point to consider when deciding to stand up or not is whether you will manage to inhibit the batsman by doing so.

Generally, the keepers have to remember that some batsmen even deliberately stand out of their ground to the medium and medium-quick bowlers in an effort to entice the keeper up close. If they succeed, they then return to their crease, comforted by the knowledge that if they manage a thick edge, the keeper is less likely to catch it and he might deflect catches to safety that first slip would have taken. Batsmen who stand out of their ground are usually front-foot players, but, as they are that much closer, the ball comes on to them more quickly and the short delivery can have them in trouble. If you find during the game that you rarely stand up to medium-pacers, you should practise against their bowling close to the stumps, so that if the occasion arises when you are needed up at the wicket, you are ready to do the job capably.

Difficult Opportunities

A way to evaluate the difficulty of a chance is to note where the ball goes after it has hit the keeper's gloves. If it drops towards the slip, gully, leg slip or even goes square of the keeper, the edge was probably so thick that the ball hit the outside of one of his gloves, or possibly just a thumb.

If for instance, the batsman achieves a thick bottom edge when cutting, the ball might only strike a keeper's fingers on the ends. Certainly these catches are the most difficult and many quite often hit part of the outside area of the catching cup formed with the gloves. But if the ball pops back out of the gloves and goes forward down the pitch, it can be assumed that it went cleanly into the cup and should have been held. Possibly the fault lay in failing to give enough to taking it. The really difficult catch standing up is again the inside edge, for you have only an instant to adjust your hands, but such chances are rare because, the ball generally goes on to the batsman's pad or body or hits the stumps.

Many unusual chances come along and a keeper must be prepared for anything. If the keeper feels he can catch a skier near the wicket and if his captain has not called, he must shout clearly mine or keeper's catch so that he can take it without fear of colliding with a colleague. The keeper should be the safest player on the field to take these catches.

STUMPING

Often people judge the difficulty of a stumping by the distance a batsman has advanced down the pitch. This in most cases is a false statement. When good players go down the wicket, they always try to ensure that the ball does not beat the outside edge of the bat by moving themselves across covering its line.

If a delivery does beat them in these circumstances, it means that they have again either player over the top or outside the line so that the ball squeezes through under the bat or between bat and pad. Again, the ball is hidden from the keeper at some stage.

As the batsman is about to play his shot, he might be only a foot out of his ground. He turns the delivery into a yorker, but the momentum of his charge takes him another two or three feet down the wicket by the time the ball arrives at the keeper.

The keeper has the time to remove the bails, but a successful stumping depends mainly on whether he re-sights the ball quickly enough to take it cleanly off this awkward full length. If the batsman pushes forward and just drags his back foot as the ball beats the outside edge, the keeper can whip off the bails and be acclaimed for a wonderful stumping, but the truth is that the keeper has been able to follow the ball all the way and with more time to see it off the pitch, since it was not far enough up for the batsman to attempt anything else but a defensive shot.

The difficulty of a stumping chance should be judged -mainly on these two points :

-was the keeper un-sighted at some state; and

where did the ball pitch.

When a batsman plays forward defensively, the bat can be as much as eight feet in front of the keeper's eyes, which gives a stumper the chance to sight and move his gloves to follow a deflection. If, however, a batsman lays back, then his bat is very close to the keeper's gloves, and he will have no chance of seeing a deflection although, unless the edge is a thick one, the ball will not have space to deviate much from its original course. Similarly with catches, many onlookers gain a false impression of the degree of difficulty, tending to base their opinion on how hard the batsman flashes at the ball.

Remember, the keeper should always be watching the ball and not a violent movement of the bat. A faint edge will produce hardly any deviation, even from a batsman who is trying to hit the ball out of the ground.

Stumping on Off-Side Deliveries

If a ball is pitched on or just outside the off-stump, it is not necessary to move more than slightly from the original stance. As the ball leaves the pitch the weight of the body is transferred to the right foot and the keeper rises from the crouching position. The fingers point to the ground and on taking the ball the body turns slightly to allow the gloves to be brought back to give with the ball. This yielding of the hands with the ball will ensure well settling of the ball into the hands. Do not try to grab at the ball.

Stumping from a ball just outside or over the off stump is effected by bringing the body well behind the line of flight of the ball. Then with a quick arm movement the bails are removed. If the ball is well wide of the off-stump the right foot must move parallel to the crease and as near to the line of flight as possible, and the left foot is taken near the right foot to keep the balance. From this well balanced position the arms are quickly swung to the stumps.

Stumping on Out-side Deliveries

One of a difficult part of wicket keeping is stumping when the delivery is made outside or over the leg stump, as the batsman's body obscures the view of the ball for a fraction of a second, as the keeper moves across to take it.

Moving speedily across to the correct position on the leg-side and accurate judgment of the course of ball off the wicket are the hallmarks of a first class wicket keeper. Whatever the type of bowler, a wicket-keeper must always adopt his normal stance.

As soon as the ball appears to be pitched outside the leg stump, keeper should take his first step across outside its line of flight, thus enabling him to take the ball on the inside of the body; this tends to make a move for stumping easier and quicker, and also gives an extra allowance, if the ball is touched, for the keeper to take the catch.

As soon as the outer foot reaches its new position the weight of the body should be transferred to it, and the other foot should then be brought across to make certain of correct balance.

Once the ball is safely taken a stumping may be made smartly removing the bails with outstretched hands.

Unusual Stumping Chances

Unusual stumping chances can occur during the game. Whenever a batsman goes down the wicket and the ball hits his pad or body be prepared to spring to the ball and return it to the wicket as quickly as possible. If the ball has rolled too far from the stumps, for the keeper to bring it back in his hands, he should flip it back. Flipping under arm is quicker than a throw over a short distance.

RUN-OUT

Run-out chances can also produce uncommon

wicket-keeping techniques. One of the most important jobs of a wicket-keeper is the taking of returns from the field, especially where a run-out is possible. Returns, many of them not accurate come at all heights and at all speeds and the man with the gloves must be very active and accurate in his catching. Returns from the field should be over the stumps and on the full, especially when a run out is attempted, otherwise, the wicket-keeper will probably find that he has to move backwards to take the ball on the bounce off the grass, or reach upwards to take the ball if it is thrown too high, or leave the stumps to take an inaccurate return.

6

RULES OF FIELDING

Cricket is a game played with a bat and ball on a large field, known as a ground, between two teams of 11 players each.

The object of the game is to score runs when at bat and to put out, or dismiss, the opposing batsmen when in the field.

The cricket rules displayed on this page here are for the traditional form of cricket which is called "Test Cricket".

However there are other formats of the game eg. 50 over matches, Twenty20 Cricket etc., where the rules differ slightly.

Player: Official Cricket Rules

Cricket is a game played between two teams made up of eleven players each. There is also a reserve player called a "twelfth man" who is used should a player be injured during play.

The twelfth man is not allowed to bowl, bat, wicket keep or captain the team. His sole duty is to act as a substiture fielder.

The original player is free to return to the game as soon as they have recovered from their injury.

To apply the law and make sure the cricket rules are upheld throughout the game there are two umpires in place during games. Umpires are responsible for making decisions and notifying the scorers of these decisions.

Two umpires are in place on the playing field while there is also a third umpire off the field who is in charge of video decisions.

This is where the call is too close for the on field umpires and they refer it to the third umpire who reviews slow motion video replays to make a decision.

Game Structure

Test cricket is a game that spans over two innings. This means that one team needs to bowl the other team out twice and score more runs then them to win the match. Another key difference between test cricket and other forms of cricket is the length of the innings. In test cricket there is no limit to the innings length. Whereas in one day cricket & Twenty20 cricket there

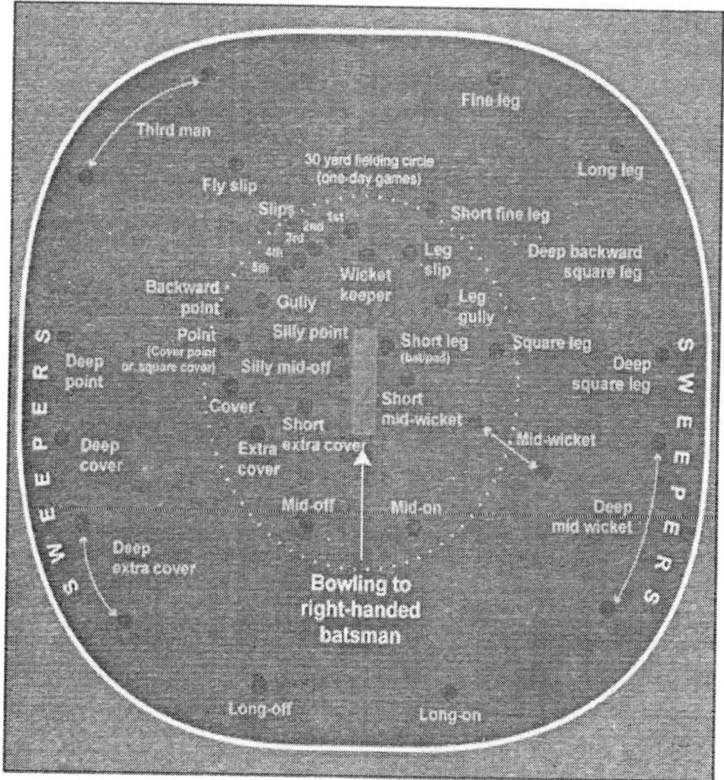

are a certain amount of overs per innings. The only limits in test cricket is a 5 day length. Before the game begins an official will toss a coin. The captain who guesses the correct side of the coin will then choose if they want to bat or field first. One team will then bat while the other will bowl & field. The aim of the batting team is to score runs while the aim of the fielding team is to bowl ten people out and close the batting teams' innings. Although there are eleven people in each team only ten people need to be bowled out as you cannot have one person batting alone. Batting is done in pairs.

Once the first team has been bowled out the second team would then go into bat. Once the second team is then bowled out it would normally return to the first team batting again. However there is an exception to this in the cricket rules, it is called the follow-on. The follow-on is when the first team makes at least 200 runs more than the second team made (in a 5 day test match). This then gives the first team the option to make the second team bat again. This is particularly useful if the game is progressing slowly or affected by bad weather and there might not be enough time for both teams to play a full innings. Should this be the case the batting team's captain also has the right to forfeit their innings at any time. This is called a declaration. Some may wonder why a captain would forfeit the opportunity for his team to bat. However if the game is coming close to a close and it looks like they will not be able to bowl the other team out again this could be an option. If one team is not bowled out twice and a winner determined in the five days of play the game is declared a draw. Therefore it may be worth declaring an innings to creat the possibility of a win rather than a draw.

Ways to Score Runs

The aim of the batsmen is to score runs. One of the main cricket rules is that for batsment to score runs they must run to each other's end of the pitch (from one end to the other). In doing this one run is scored. Cricket rules state they may run multiple runs per shot. As well as running they can also score runs by hitting boundaries. A boundary scores the batsmen either 4 or 6 runs. A four is scored by hitting the ball past the boundary after hitting the groud while a six is scored by hitting the ball past the boundary on the full (before it hits the ground). Cricket rules also state that once a 4 or 6 has been scored any runs physically ran by the batsman are null & void. They will only obtain the 4 or 6 runs.

Other ways runs can be scored according to the cricket rules include no balls, wide balls, byes & leg byes. Cricket rules state that all runs scored by these methods are awarded to the batting team but not the individual batters.

- A "No Ball" can be declared for many reasons: If the bowler bowls the ball from the wrong place, the ball is declared dangerous (often happens when bowled at the batsmen's body on the full), bounces more than twice or rolls before reaching the batsman or if fielders are standing in illegal positions. The batsman can hit a no ball and score runs off it but cannot be out from a no ball except if they are ran out, hit the ball twice, handle the ball or obstruct the field. The batsman gains any runs scored off the no ball for his shot while the team also gains one run for the no ball itself.
- A "Wide Ball" will be declared if the umpire thinks the batsman did not have a reasonable opportunity to score off the delivery. However if the delivery is bowled over the batsmen's head it will not be declared a wide but a no ball. Umpires are much stricter on wide deliveries in the shorter format of the game while being much more relaxed in test cricket. A wide delivery will add one run to the batting team and any runs scored by the batsman. The batsman is not able to get out off a

wide delivery except if they are stumped, run out, handle the ball, hit their wicket or obstruct the field.

• A "Bye" is where a ball that isn't a no ball or wide passes the striking batsman and runs are scored without the batsman hitting the ball.

• A "Leg Bye" is where runs are scored by hitting the batsman, but not the bat and the ball is not a no ball or wide. However no runs can be scored if the striking batsman didn't attempt to play a shot or if he was avoiding the ball.

Ways Batsmen can be given out according to cricket rules

There are a number of different ways a batsman can be given out in the game of cricket. When a bowler gets a batsman out it is said that the bowler gets a "wicket". Following are the different ways a batsman can be given out according to the rules of cricket:

• **Bowled** - Cricket rules state that if the ball is bowled and hits the striking batsman's wickets the batsman is given out (as long as at least one bail is removed by the ball). It does not matter whether the ball has touched the batsman's bat, gloves, body or any other part of the batsman. However the ball is not allowed to have touched another player or umpire before hitting the wickets.

• **Caught** - Cricket rules state that if a batsman hits the ball or touches the ball at all with his bat or hand/ glove holding the bat then the batsman can be caught out. This is done by the fielders, wicket keeper or bowler catching the ball on the full (before it bounces). If this is done then cricket rules state the batsman is out.

• **Leg Before Wicket (LBW)** - If the ball is bowled and it hits the batsman first without the bat hitting it then an LBW decision is possible. However for the umpire to give this out he must first look at some of the factors stated in the cricket rules. The first thing the umpire need to decide is would the ball have hit the wickets if the batsman was not there. If his answer to this is yes and the ball was not pitched on the leg side of the wicket he can safely give the batsman out. However if the ball hits the batsman outside the line of off stump while he was attempting to play a stroke then he is not out.

• **Stumped** - A batsman can be given out according to cricket rules when the wicketkeeper puts down his wicket while he is out of his crease and not attempting a run (if he is attempting a run it would be a runout).

• **Run Out** - Cricket rules state that a batsman is out if no part of his bat or body is grounded behind the popping crease while the ball is in play and the wicket is fairly put down by the fielding side.

• **Hit Wicket** - Cricket rules specify that if a batsman hits his wicket down with his bat or body after the bowler has entered his delivery stried and the ball is in play then he is out. The striking batsman is also out if he hits his wicket down while setting off for his first run.

• **Handled The Ball** - Cricket rules allow the batsman to be given out if he willingly handles the ball with the hand that is not touching the bat without the consent of the opposition.

• **Timed Out** - An incoming batsman must be ready to face a ball or be at the non strikers end with his partner within three minutes of the outgoing batsman being dismissed. If this is not done the incoming batsman can be given out.

• **Hit The Ball Twice** - Cricket rules state that if a batsman hits a ball twice other than for the purpose of protecting his wicket or with consent from the opposition he is out.

• **Obstructing The Field** - A batsman is out if he willingly obstructs the opposition by word or action

There are many other cricket rules. However these are most of the basics and will get you well on your way to playing the game. Many of the more advanced rules & laws can be learned along the way and are not vital to general play.

Fielding Positions

Fielders assist the bowlers to prevent batsmen from scoring too many runs. There are several types of field positions and the captain of the fielding team decides different combinations of them for tactical reasons. Since there are 11 players on a team, one of whom is the bowler and another the wicket-keeper, at most nine other fielding positions can be used at any given time. The captain may move players between fielding positions at any time except when a bowler is in the act of bowling to a batsman.

Wicket Keeper

The wicketkeeper who stands behind the batsman on strike at the wicket, sets the tone for the fielding side. His role is to stop balls that pass the batsman and attempt to dismiss the batsman in various ways.

First Slip

Most important fielding position in the game. The fielder at First slip, normally stands closest to the wicketkeeper.

Second Slip

The fielder at Second slip stands just to the offside of first slip. The second slip is likely to be used in the first couple of over's of a match or if a team is employing an attacking field in an attempt to finish an innings off.

Gully

The Gully fielder covers the area just square of the wicket on the off side but the fielder will tend to vary where they stand according to the pitch and the batsman. Gully is employed in catching the ball after it hits the edge of the bat and deflects a long way, or for misplaced cut shots.

Third Man

This is a boundary position right behind square on the offside. The fielder at Third man has to covers a large area, preventing anything that pierces the slip and gully area.

Point

A position on the off side and located at 90 degrees to the batsman. The Point fielder's job is to catch the ball from a misplaced cut shot, or to prevent runs from cut shots, square drives, and defensive strokes square on the off side.

Cover Point

This is the fielding position on the off side in front of the wicket.

Deep Point

Deep point is a defensive position on the off side and the fielder at this position is usually stationed on the boundary.

Cover

This is fielding position in front of the wicket and the position designed to prevent runs from cover drives, defensive strokes on the off side.

Extra Cover

This is the fielding position in front of the wicket. A strong off side field would probably have both a cover and an extra cover.

Sweeper

This is the fielding position in the deep outfield near the boundary used when the fielding side wants to keep the runs to the bare minimum.

Silly Mid Off

This is the fielding position on the off side, and the position is almost mid way to the wicket and very close to the batsman.

Mid Off

This is the fielding position on the off side, and the position is almost straight in line with the bat to prevent runs from off drives, and defensive strokes on the off side.

Long Off

A fielding position on the off side and has to cover a large area from the sight screen to the sweeper cover position and near the boundary to prevent runs from off drives or catch long, lofted off drives.

Long On

A fielding position on the leg side of the wicket to

prevent runs from on drives or catch long, lofted on drives.

Mid On

A fielding position on the leg side almost straight of the batsman to prevent runs from on drives, and defensive strokes on the on side

Mid Wicket

This is positioned on the leg side and the position is designed generally to either catch the ball from a misplaced pull shot, or to prevent runs from on drives, and defensive strokes on the on side.

Deep Mid Wicket

This is positioned on the leg side near the boundary to prevent boundaries.

Silly Mid On

This is positioned on the leg side forward of the strikers wicket and very close to the batsmen generally use to put pressure on them.

Short Leg

A fielding position to the right of forward square leg and very close to the batsman. This position usually given to the youngest member of the fielding side and employed against players who are especially strong off their hips.

Backward Short Leg

This position is similar to first slip on the leg side and is very often referred to as leg slip.

Square Leg

This position is on the leg side. This is also the position for the leg umpire. Between the wicket and the square boundary, it prevents the batsman from going for pull shots.

Deep / Backward Square Leg

This position can also be monitored by the fielders from the deep mid wicket and deep fine leg regions.

Fine Leg

This is the fielding position on the leg side to the right of the square leg region designed to catch the ball from a misplaced bock or other defensive shot.

7

CRICKET TERMINOLOGIES

Across the line

A batsman plays across the line when he moves his bat in a direction lateral to the direction of the incoming ball.

Appeal

the act of a bowler or fielder shouting at the umpire to ask if his last ball took the batsman's wicket. Usually phrased in the form of howzat. Common variations include 'Howzee?', or simply turning to the umpire and shouting. The umpire cannot give a batsman out unless the fielding side appeals, even if the criteria for a dismissal have otherwise been met. However, batsmen who are obviously out will normally leave the field without waiting for an appeal.

Attacking field

A fielding configuration in which more fielders are close in to the pitch so as to take catches and dismiss batsmen more readily, at the risk of letting more runs get scored should the ball get past them.

Bodyline

a tactic (now suppressed by law changes restricting fielders on the leg side) involving bowling directly at the batsman's body, particularly with close fielders packed on the leg side. Bodyline was a common tactic in the contentious 1932–33 Ashes Tour. The tactic is often called "fast leg theory" in other contexts.

Boot Hill

Another term for short leg, the least liked and most dangerous of the fielding positions.

Bottom hand

The hand of the batsman that is closest to the blade of the bat. Shots played with the bottom hand often are hit in the air.

Bowl-out

a method of determining the result in a Twenty 20 match that has been tied. Five players from each team bowl at a full set of stumps, and the team with the most hits wins. If the number of hits is equal after both team's turns, further sudden death turns are taken. The concept is analogous to the penalty shootout used in other sports.

Box

a protective item shaped like a half-shell and inserted into the front pouch of a jockstrap worn underneath a player's (particularly a batsman's) trousers to protect his or her genitalia from the hard cricket ball. Also known as an 'abdominal protector', 'Hector protector', 'ball box', 'protector' or 'cup'.

Bunsen

A pitch on which spin bowlers can turn the ball prodigiously. From the rhyming slang: 'Bunsen Burner' meaning 'Turner'.

Call

1. The act of a fieldsman in announcing to other fieldsmen that he is in a position to take a catch, usually by shouting the word "mine". This is considered good practice, as it prevents two fieldsmen colliding with one another in an attempt to take the same catch. See mine.

2. Calling is the process by which a batsman announces to his partner whether or not to take a run. A batsman is said to have the call if it is his responsibility

to announce to his batting partner whether or not to take a run. Generally, the call is taken by the batting partner who has the better view of the ball: by the striker for a shot forward of the crease, or the non-striker for a shot behind square. Only one batsman makes a call to avoid errors which would lead to a run out.

Cap

headwear traditionally worn by cricketers in the field.

Carry

if a hit ball is caught by a fielder on the fly, it is said to have carried. If it bounces just short of the fielder, it is said not to have carried. The carry of a delivery to the wicket keeper is also noted as a measure of the quality of the pitch.

Carry the Bat

an opener who is not out at the end of a completed innings is said to have carried his bat.

Cart-wheeling stump

when a ball hits a stump with enough force to cause it to make vertical revolutions before landing.

Caught and bowled

when a player is dismissed by a catch taken by the bowler. The term originates from the way dismissals are recorded on a scorecard; the alternative "bowled and caught", referring to the sequence of events in the chronological order, is almost never used.

Caught behind

a catch by the wicket-keeper.

Chuck

to throw the ball instead of bowling it (i.e. by straightening the elbow during the delivery); also chucker: a bowler who chucks; and chucking: such an illegal bowling action. All are considered offensive terms as they imply cheating.

Circle

a painted circle (or ellipse), centred in the middle of the pitch, of radius 30-yard (27 m) marked on the field. The circle separates the infield from the outfield, used in policing the fielding regulations in certain one-day versions of the game. The exact nature of the restrictions vary depending on the type of game: see limited overs cricket, Twenty20 and powerplay (cricket).

Corridor of uncertainty

a good line. The corridor of uncertainty is a notional narrow area on and just outside a batsman's off stump. If a delivery is in the corridor, it is difficult for a batsman to decide whether to leave the ball, play defensively or play an attacking shot. The term was popularised by former England batsman, now commentator, Geoffrey Boycott.

Fall of wicket

the batting team's score at which a batsman gets out. Often abbreviated to "FoW" in scorecards.

Fielder

a player on the fielding side who is neither the bowler nor the wicket-keeper, in particular one who has just fielded the ball.

Fine

of a position on the field behind the batsman, closer to the line of the pitch (wicket-to-wicket); the opposite of square.

Flat pitch

a pitch which is advantageous to the batsmen and offers little or no help to the bowlers, due to predictable bounce.

Green top

a pitch with an unusually high amount of visible grass, that might be expected to assist the pace bowlers.

In/out field

a field setting, usually with 5 close fielders and 3 on the boundary, designed to force batsmen into errors by trying to deny the opportunity to score singles while saving easy boundaries.

Infield

the region of the field that lies inside the 30-yard circle (27 m) or, in the days before defined circles, the area of the field close to the wicket bounded by an imaginary line through square leg, mid on, mid off and cover point.

Mis-field

a fielder failing to collect the ball cleanly, often fumbling a pick-up or dropping a catch.

Obstructing the field

a match in which one side has more players than the other. Generally the extra players were allowed to field as well as bat and so the bowling side had more than 11 fielders.

Outfield

the part of the field lying outside the 30-yard (27 m) circle measured from the centre of the pitch or, less formally, the part of the pitch furthest from the wickets.

Pitch

1. the rectangular surface in the centre of the field where most of the action takes place, usually made of earth or clay. It is 22 yards in length.
2. of the ball, to bounce before reaching the batsman after delivery.
3. the spot where the ball pitches (sense 2).

Point

A fielding position square of the batsman's off side.

Popping crease

One of two lines in the field defined as being four feet in front of and parallel to that end's bowling crease where the wickets are positioned. A batsman who does not have either the bat or some part of his or her body touching the ground behind the popping crease is considered out of his ground and is in danger of being dismissed run out or stumped.

Ring field

A field which is set primarily to save singles, consisting of fieldsmen in all or most of the primary positions forward of the wicket, on or about the fielding circle (or where it would be).

Road

A very hard and flat pitch, good for batting on. Synonyms such as street, highway, etc. may sometimes be used in the same context.

Roller

a cylindrical implement used to flatten the pitch before play.

Rotate the strike

to look to make singles wherever possible, in order to ensure that both batsmen are continually facing deliveries and making runs. The opposite of farming the strike.

Rough

a worn-down section of the pitch, often due to bowlers' footmarks, from which spinners are able to obtain more turn.

Roundarm bowling

the type of bowling action in which the bowler's outstretched hand is perpendicular to his body when he releases the ball. Round arm bowling is legal in cricket.

Run chase

The act/task of the team batting second (in a limited-overs match) or batting fourth (in an unlimited overs match), trying to win a match by batting and surpassing the runs accumulated by the opponent.

Run out

dismissal by a member of the fielding side breaking the wicket while the batsman is outside his/her crease in the process of making a run.

Run rate

the average number of runs scored per over.

Runner

a player from the batting side who assists an injured batsman by running between the wickets. The runner wears and carry the same equipment, and can be run out. Since 2011, runners have not been permitted in international cricket, but can be used at lower grades.

Selector

a person who is delegated with the task of choosing players for a cricket team. Typically the term is used in the context of player selection for national, provincial and other representative teams at the professional levels of the game, where a "panel of selectors" acts under the authority of the relevant national or provincial cricket administrative body.

Session

A period of play, from start to lunch, lunch to tea and tea until stumps.

Short-pitched

a delivery that bounces relatively close to the bowler. The intent is to make the ball bounce well above waist height (a bouncer). A slow or low-bouncing short-pitched ball is known as a long hop.

Shot Stop

When the wicket keeper stands upfront, the fielder placed right behind the wicket keeper is called a Shot Stop. When the fielder stands outside the 30-yard circle he is called a Long Stop.

Slash

a cut, but played aggressively or possibly recklessly

– a cut (q.v.) being a shot played square on the off side to a short-pitched delivery wide of off stump. So called because the batsman makes a "cutting" motion as he plays the shot.

Slice

a kind of cut shot played with the bat making an obtuse angle with the batsman.

Slip

a close fielder behind the batsman, next to the wicket-keeper on the off-side. Also ("in the slips", "at first slip") the positions occupied by such fielders. Commonly there will be two or three slips in an attacking field (although there is no limit and a captain may use more), and one or none in a defensive field. A specialist slip fieldsman may be known as a slipper.

Standing up

position adopted by a Wicket-keeper, close to the stumps, when a slow (or, occasionally, medium pace) bowler is operating.

Street

a pitch which is easy for batsmen and difficult for bowlers. Sometimes called a road, highway, and various other synonyms for street.

Stump

1. one of the three vertical posts making up the wicket ("off stump", "middle stump" and "leg stump");
2. a way of dismissing a batsman; or
3. ("stumps") or ("at stumps") the end of a day's play.

Substitute (cricket)